THE HISTORY DETECTIVE INVESTIGATES

BRITAIN AT WAR
RATIONING

Martin Parsons

D0185606

Editor: Jason Hook
Designer: Simon Borrough
Cartoon artwork: Richard Hook

This book is dedicated to Alistair Borthwick and Callum Parsons. May they never have to experience the effects of wartime rationing. The author would like to thank Ruth Mott for kindly allowing the use of her wartime recipes and personal reminiscences.

First published in 1999 by Wayland Publishers Ltd, 61 Western Rd, Hove, East Sussex, BN3 1JD ©
Copyright 1999 Wayland Publishers Ltd
This edition published in 2000 by Wayland Publishers Ltd
Find Wayland on the Internet at http://www.wayland.co.uk

British Library Cataloguing in Publication Data
Parsons, Martin
  Rationing. – (The history detective investigates. Britain at war)
  1. World War 1939-1945 – Food supply – Great Britain – Juvenile literature
  2. Rationing – Great Britain – History – 20th century – Juvenile literature
  3. World War, 1939-1945 – Social aspects – Great Britain – Juvenile literature
  I. Title   II. Hook, Richard 941'084

ISBN 0 7502 2846 6

Printed and bound in Italy by G. Canale & C. SpA., Turin
Cover pictures: (bottom) a fishmonger checks shoppers' identity cards in 1943; (top-centre) canned food from wartime; (top-right) a poster encouraging people to grow their own food.
Title page: Pigs being reared on scraps by the council in 1940.

Picture Acknowledgements: The publishers would like to thank the following for permission to reproduce their pictures: Getty Images *cover* (bottom), *title page*, 4, 8 (top), 11 (bottom), 13 (top), 16 (right), 18 (bottom), 20 (bottom), 21 (top), 22 (bottom), 23 (bottom), 25 (bottom), 26 (bottom), 29 (bottom-left); Imperial War Museum, London 14 (top), 15 (bottom); John Frost Historical Newspapers 5 (right), 8 (bottom), 9 (bottom), 22 (top), 24 (bottom), 29 (bottom-right); Peter Newark's Historical Pictures *cover* (top-right), 5 (left), 9 (top-left), 10 (top), 12 (bottom), 13 (bottom); Popperfoto 10 (bottom), 12 (top), 15 (top), 24 (top), 28; Public Record Office 17, 18 (top), 21 (bottom), 23 (top), 25 (top), 27 (top), 29 (top); Robin Holyoake 16 (left); Science & Society Picture Library 7 (right), 14 (bottom), 19, 27 (bottom); Topham 6 (bottom), 9 (top-right); Wayland Picture Library, photography by Rupert Horrox, courtesy of the Imperial War Museum, London *cover* (top-centre), 6 (top), 10 (centre-right), 11 (top); Wayland Picture Library 20 (top). Logo artwork by John Yates.

All Wayland books encourage children to read and help them improve their literacy.

✓ The contents page, page numbers, headings and index help locate specific pieces of information.

✓ The glossary reinforces alphabetic knowledge and extends vocabulary.

✓ The further information section suggests other books dealing with the same subject.

✓ Find out more about how this book is specifically relevant to the National Literacy Strategy on page 30.

CONTENTS

RATIONING

As the Second World War began, German submarines left their ports and slid beneath the waves. Soon they were in the North Atlantic, searching for the ships that carried vital supplies to Britain from the USA and Canada. As the months passed, ship after ship was torpedoed and sunk. Thousands of tonnes of food, fuel and machinery went to the bottom of the sea.

Before the war, much of Britain's food had been brought in from overseas. Half the country's meat and most of its cheese, sugar, fruit and wheat were imported. When these vital supplies were cut off, food had to be rationed. What did people eat? How did rationing work? What other products were rationed, apart from food? There are many clues to tell us. By finding these clues, we can discover how people learnt to cope with rationing.

The first boatload of bananas (above) reaches Britain after the war, on 28 January 1946. During the war, it was almost impossible to obtain bananas.

A convoy (below) carrying vital supplies to Britain. Despite being protected by warships, many cargo ships were sunk by German submarines.

The history detective Sherlock Bones will help you to find clues in newspapers, photographs, posters, recipe books and other documents. You should then be able to find enough evidence to present a project on rationing. Sherlock's own project is to investigate how people fed their pets during rationing. You can see the clues he discovers on page 29.

Wherever you see one of Sherlock's paw-prints, like this, you will find a puzzle to solve. The answers can all be found on page 31.

Look at the newspaper and the poster.
- What foods were rationed at the start of the war?
- What types of ration books were issued?
- What do you think 'Dig for Victory' means? You can find some clues on page 18.

In 1940 the 'Dig for Victory' slogan was introduced. The foot in the picture belonged to Mr W. H. McKie of Acton, London. It was printed millions of times on leaflets and posters.

This newspaper, published at the start of the war, shows how little butter people were allowed to buy.

DAILY EXPRESS. Thursday, November 2, 1939.

Daily Express

WORLD'S LARGEST DAILY SALE

"OIL" CLEAR — K.C.C. DRUMS — E. A. BROUGH & CO. LIVERPOOL 8

BLACK-OUT ZERO HOUR TO-NIGHT UNTIL 7.57 A.M.

No. 12,309   Thursday, November 2, 1939

Here is your BUTTER ration (actual size) for a week

SUNDAY   MONDAY   TUESDAY   WEDNESDAY   THURSDAY   FRIDAY   SATURDAY

HAM, TOO

And this is how far it goes—

Half a coupon for a ham sandwich

But none for butter in a restaurant

WHEN BUTTER AND BACON ARE RATIONED, HAM WILL BE RATIONED, TOO.

The rations announced last night will probably begin on December 16. They will be a quarter of a pound each of butter and bacon for every individual. That means a pound of bacon and a pound of butter for a family of four.

Ham will be treated as part of the bacon ration; bacon coupons will have to be given up from your ration book when you buy ham.

Margarine will not be rationed. Nor will pork, sausages, meat, or any other food—yet.

There will be three kinds of ration books—a general one for men, women and children over six years old; a child's book for children under six; and a traveller's book for people who do not permanently live at home.

RATIONS The answers to your questions

Butter ration is a quarter of a pound weekly. That is enough, each day, to spread thinly five slices of bread—each four by three inches.

Here's your week's BACON

Bacon ration is a quarter of a pound a week. Four slices—each a tenth of an inch thick. Four-sevenths of a rasher a day. In the picture, left, is a side view of a ration rasher "life-size."

Treasure, 'spy' girl found

4 a.m. EDITION

Finland mines port Soviet wants

"Independence is not for sale"

COPENHAGEN, Thursday Morning.

MINES have been laid at Hangoe, Finnish port at the mouth of the Gulf of Finland which the Soviet wishes to be ceded to her, announces the Finnish Legation in Copenhagen.

The channel between the islands of Hastus and Busoe has been closed.—British United Press.

Finland answered back over the radio late last night to the "malicious attacks made on the Finnish State in Soviet broadcasts.

Speaking in Russian from a station near the frontier, the announcer said Finland could never agree to a past such as Stalin has forced on smaller Baltic nations.

Finland's Foreign Minister, Dr. Erkko, also broadcast to the Finnish people and to the 100,000 Finnish Army on the frontier that Finland's independence was not for sale.

"Stalin's demands," he declared, "may be a small thing to a great nation like Russia, but to us they are very big indeed.

"A way out and must be found for Finland and Russia to live together, but no pressure can change our resolution. The country is determined to defend itself."

You can see the clues he discovers on page 29. The answers can all be found on page 31. You can find some clues on page 18.

RATION BOOKS

ON HIS MAJESTY'S
SERVICE.

OFFICIAL PAID

This cover must not be detached from this Ration Book.

Consumer's Name: *Lamb J Sybil*
Address: *100 New Park Rd*
Clapham Park
S.W.2

OPEN CAREFULLY

AXCW
43
Serial Number of Book: *2*

Date of Issue
2 3 OCT 1939

IF FOUND, RETURN TO
WANDSWORTH
FOOD OFFICE.
R.B.T. [General]

AC 940666

This ration book was issued to Sybil Lamb in Clapham Park, London.

❧ When was the ration book (above) issued?

The government was worried that as food became scarcer, prices would rise and poorer people might be unable to afford to eat. There was also a danger that some people would hoard food, leaving none for others. Eventually, Britain might be starved into surrender. To prevent this happening, the government introduced rationing, so that everyone could get a fair share of the food available.

National Registration Day took place on 29 September 1939. Every householder had to fill in a form giving details of the people who lived in their house. Using this information, the government issued everyone with an identity card and a ration book.

A shopkeeper cuts out coupons from a customer's ration book on 8 January 1940, known as 'Coupon Monday', when the rationing of butter, bacon and ham began.

MINISTRY OF FOOD

YOUR NEW RATION BOOK

HOW TO REGISTER WITH THE SHOPS

The new Ration Books are now being distributed. As soon as you receive your new Book you must fill in the particulars as explained below, and then take the Book to the shops for fresh Registration. It has been found possible to allow *immediate* Registration, and the sooner you register the better. This is what to do :—

1 On the pages of coupons for Rationed Foods (Meat, Bacon, Butter and Sugar) you must fill in your name and address ('BLOCK LETTERS) in the space provided in the centre of each page.

2 At the foot of these pages are spaces marked 'Counterfoil'. Here you must write your name and address, the date, and the name and address of the shop where you wish to buy the particular food during the six months' period beginning July 8th.

3 Inside the front cover of your Ration Book you must write the names and addresses of the shops.

4 As soon as you have done this, take the Book to each of the shops with whom you intend to register, so that they may cut out their counterfoils.

EVERYONE MUST REGISTER FOR THE NEW PERIOD

This notice appeared in newspapers telling people how to register with their local shops so that they could receive their rations.

🐾 The notice above explains that the shopkeeper will cut the coupons out of the ration book. Later, the system was changed and the shopkeeper just drew a line through a smaller coupon. Can you guess why this change was made?

In November 1939 everybody was warned that butter and bacon would soon be rationed, and told to register with a local shopkeeper. Food rationing began on 8 January 1940. When a shopper purchased their ration of food, the shopkeeper cut the coupons out of their ration book to show that they had received their allowance. Each person was allowed to buy 4 ounces (113 g) of butter, and 4 ounces (113 g) of bacon or ham per week. Sugar was also rationed. People were allowed no more than 12 ounces (340 g) each week.

NATIONAL BUTTER RATION COUPONS TODAY

A customer gives her ration book to a shopkeeper on 'Coupon Monday'.

DETECTIVE WORK
Try to find a ration book in a junk shop, or at a car-boot or jumble sale. A member of your family might even still have one. Find as many clues as you can in the ration book. Who owned it? When was it issued? What food could be bought with it?

SHOPPING

People bought their food at the shops where they were registered. There were no supermarkets, so people had to visit several different shops to buy meat, vegetables, bread and other goods. In each shop, customers had to wait their turn to be served by the shopkeeper, and sometimes they would get to the counter and find there was nothing left. Going shopping became a tiring and often disappointing experience.

This shop would only sell its fish to local shoppers.

12 OZ. OF SUGAR A WEEK FROM JAN. 8

MEAT ALSO TO BE RATIONED, PROBABLY IN FEBRUARY

The extension of food rationing to include sugar and meat as well as butter, bacon and ham was announced last night by the Ministry of Food.

Sugar rationing will start on Monday week, Jan. 8. The allowance will be 12oz a week for each person.

A newspaper warning that rationing will be extended to meat and sugar.

❖ Why does the notice on the shop in the photograph above ask for customers' identity cards?

As the war went on, more and more ships carrying supplies to Britain were sunk. Rationing had to be extended to other foods and the rations also became smaller. The newspaper story on the left was published on 29 December 1939, just before rationing was introduced. It warned that other foods were to be rationed.

Rationing was organized by the Ministry of Food. This government department was divided into different sections, such as the Potato and Carrot Division and the Bacon and Ham Division.

This painting shows the weekly rations for two people in 1941.

Ration books with cheese coupons.

The Ministry of Food extended rationing further to include cheese, cooking fat and tea. Some foods, such as bread, were never rationed. But it became very difficult to find other foods, such as bananas and oranges. These were brought in by ship before the war, but during the war ships could carry only essential supplies.

YOUR SUGAR allowance of three-quarters of a pound is about 25 per cent less than what is used in normal times.

If you make marmalade you will still be able to get extra sugar – 3 lb to every 2 lb of oranges.

GUARANTEED

But you will have to prove that you have bought the oranges for marmalade-making by producing 'documentary evidence' such as an invoice.

Such evidence will earn you a permit at your local food office, and you will give the permit to your grocer.

There will be special allowances for manufacturing purposes such as for sweets, chocolate, cakes.

Beekeepers, too, will be allowed 10 lb per hive for feeding their bees between now and the end of May.

DETECTIVE WORK

Visit your local library and ask to look at wartime newspapers on microfilm. Look through newspapers for 1940 and 1941. Try to find headlines about the Ministry of Food, and the rationing of different foods.

Look at the newspaper article above, from December 1939. How could people get an extra ration of sugar?

NEW FOODS

In 1941, new food products began to appear on the shelves. Many were carried by ships which crossed the Atlantic in armed convoys from the USA. There was tinned meat called Spam. There was a shortage of eggs, so powdered egg was shipped in. When American troops arrived in Britain to join the war effort, they brought supplies of chewing gum, cigarettes and sweets.

People soon got used to tinned and dried foods. Spam was eaten cold in sandwiches, mashed to make shepherd's pie or fried for breakfast. Tinned sausage meat from the USA was surrounded in the tin by a layer of fat which could be used to make pastry. Tins of dried eggs were available as rations after June 1942. One tablespoon of powered egg was added to two tablespoons of water to make the equivalent of one real egg.

An advertisement for Spam, from November 1939.

A selection of tinned foods. Can you see the tinned eggs?

A queue of shoppers in February 1941, waiting to buy eggs. Notice the woman coming out holding her one egg.

A selection of tinned foods. Can you see the dried skimmed milk from the USA?

People sometimes became very suspicious about exactly what food they were eating, as the quote below from one of Sherlock's interviews tells us.

'Mum had managed to get a tin of pineapple for tea – I'd never tasted pineapple before and we were all looking forward to it. Grandad took one mouthful and spat it straight out. He was convinced it was turnip! I'm not sure whether it was or not, but it put me off tinned pineapple for life.'

Alan Cooper,
recalling his wartime childhood.

Unusual foods were served up at special occasions. People who were getting married could apply for extra rations, but they did not get very much. The shortage of eggs made it difficult to bake cakes, and in August 1940 the Ministry of Food banned the use of icing on wedding cakes. Some people made cardboard covers decorated with crêpe paper and flowers, which could be put over the top of an ordinary cake.

DETECTIVE WORK

At your local reference library, ask to look at the street directories for the 1940s. Make a copy of any advertisements which promote new products, or those from the USA.

American film actress Carole Landis and her husband cut a sultana cake disguised as a wedding cake at the Savoy Hotel, London.

'DON'T WASTE IT!'

The government launched a propaganda campaign telling people to use their rations carefully. It was very important to avoid waste because so many merchant ships were being sunk. Also, British factories could no longer produce large quantities of goods such as clothes and toiletries. Many factory workers had been called up into the armed forces, and those who remained were needed to produce armaments.

Factories produced essential goods, not luxuries. These women are working in a steel factory in November 1943.

The 'Squander Bug' appeared on many posters.

🐾 What is the symbol that appears on the Squander Bug and why do you think it was used?

Posters and notices in newspapers explained that people could help the war effort by avoiding waste and buying only essential items. A cartoon character called the 'Squander Bug' was used in campaigns against waste. These suggested that people who bought luxuries instead of saving their money were helping the enemy to win the war.

A housewife uses her ration book to buy some essential items.

If you look in wartime newspapers, you will see that they joined in the campaign. Some published quizzes all about saving waste and recycling.

DORSET COUNTY CHRONICLE AND SWANAGE TIMES,
23 DECEMBER 1943

Does Mother know her Ps and Qs?

1 Which of these is the correct way to wash cooking fat so that it can be used again?

a) Pour boiling water over it.

b) Rub through a fine sieve.

c) Bring to the boil in water, pour into a bowl, when cool, lift off and scrape underneath.

d) Hold it under running water.

Answer: C

Many manufacturers produced advertisements like the one below, claiming that their products saved waste. They suggested that housewives would be 'doing their bit' for the war effort by using them.

WASH FOR VICTORY

Thrifty housewives save money. Thanks to Oxydol's amazing extra lather you can do twice as much washing for your money.

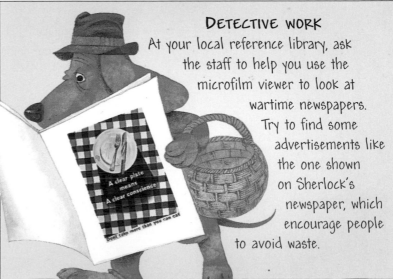

DETECTIVE WORK
At your local reference library, ask the staff to help you use the microfilm viewer to look at wartime newspapers. Try to find some advertisements like the one shown on Sherlock's newspaper, which encourage people to avoid waste.

STAYING HEALTHY

People had to get used to eating less food and to going without certain foods. Scientists in the Ministry of Food had to make sure that everyone ate enough of the right foods – such as fruits and vegetables – to stay healthy during rationing.

An advertisement using the cartoon character Doctor Carrot. His message was that people should eat carrots, because they are healthy.

DOCTOR CARROT
*guards
your Health*

VIT-A

Vegetables were cheap, easy to grow and full of vitamins. To persuade people to eat more vegetables, the Ministry of Food created advertisements featuring cartoon characters. These included Potato Pete, Clara Carrot, Carroty George and Doctor Carrot. Carrots contain Vitamin A, which was believed to help people see in the dark.

✿ Why was it important for people to be able to see well in the dark during the war?

This photograph of a boy buying an orange on 20 October 1941 is full of clues about rationing and staying healthy.

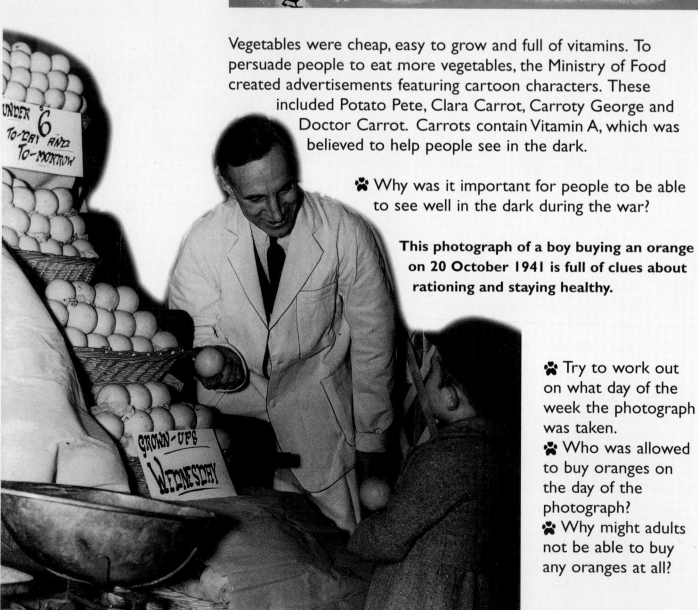

UNDER 6
TO-DAY AND
TO-MORROW

GROWN-UPS
WEDNESDAY

✿ Try to work out on what day of the week the photograph was taken.
✿ Who was allowed to buy oranges on the day of the photograph?
✿ Why might adults not be able to buy any oranges at all?

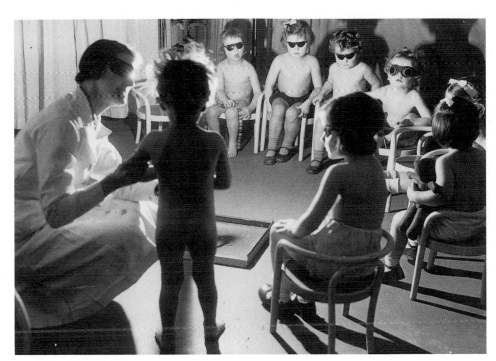

These children are receiving sun-ray treatment in a health centre in Finsbury, London, in November 1942.

MINISTRY OF FOOD

CHEAP MILK

for
Mothers & Children

The National Milk Scheme provides one pint of milk a day, at a reduced price or free, for every expectant or nursing mother and every child under five not attending school.

● Get an Application Form from the Milk Officer at your local Food Office (the Post Office will give you the address); or through any Child Welfare Centre, Health Visitor or District Nurse.

● Fill in the top half of the Application Form and then have it signed by a responsible person (such as a Teacher or Clergyman), who knows you well.

● In the case of an expectant mother, the form must also be signed by a Doctor, Certified Midwife or Health Visitor.

● Post the form to the local Food Office. It will be about ten days before you receive your Milk Permit.

MILK AT 2d. PER PINT

● All expectant and nursing mothers, and children under five not attending school, will be able to get milk at 2d. per pint.

In December 1941 the government introduced the Vitamin Welfare Scheme, to make sure that children could get the vitamins they needed to stay healthy. Babies up to the age of two were given blackcurrant syrup which contains vitamin C. They also received cod-liver oil, containing vitamins A and D, free of charge.

Later in the war, children received orange juice rather than blackcurrant syrup, and the scheme was widened to cover all pregnant women and children under five. They also received free or cheap milk, as you can see from the document on this page.

There were reasons other than rationing why children needed extra vitamins. The children in the amazing photograph above were given sun-ray treatment to increase their levels of Vitamin D – which comes from sunlight. Children had this treatment because they had spent so long in the darkness of air-raid shelters.

The notice above was printed in newspapers, and informed people about how to obtain free or cheap milk.

❧ Look at the document carefully. Who could sign the application form of an expectant mother?

DETECTIVE WORK
At your local reference library, look in wartime newspapers for pictures of Potato Pete (shown above) and the Carrot characters. Make copies of them, and try to design your own cartoon to advertise other vegetables in the same style.

STRANGE RECIPES

People got used to eating all sorts of strange foods. Some recipes required ingredients that were no longer available, so substitutes had to be found. The Ministry of Food and organizations like the Women's Institute produced recipe books full of ideas. Recipes were also broadcast on a popular radio programme called *The Kitchen Front*.

A cook demonstrates how to cook potato and leek soup, and hamburger steaks with brussel sprouts. The women have been given printed recipes, which you can see them holding in their hands.

❁ What posters can you see on the wall?

Today many people are vegetarians, but at the time of the Second World War most people liked to have meat with their meals. Because meat was rationed, many new wartime recipes replaced meat with vegetables. 'Lord Woolton pie' was named after the Minister of Food and contained potatoes, swede, cauliflower and spring onions. The health of the nation actually improved during the war, because people ate more vegetables.

This is the cover of a booklet containing some of the recipes broadcast on the radio programme *The Kitchen Front*.

Potatoes and carrots were the surprise ingredients in a whole range of dishes, replacing fruit in sweet recipes like the one below.

PORTMAN PUDDING

6 oz flour, 4 oz grated raw carrot and potato, teaspoon mixed spice,
2 tablespoons sugar, 1 level teaspoon bicarbonate of soda, a pinch of salt,
1/2 cupful sultanas and raisins, 2 oz fat.

Cream the fat and sugar, add carrot, potato, flour, spice and soda. Mix well. Add fruit. Add water if necessary to make a soft dropping consistency. Steam for 2 hours at least. Serves 3 or 4. A sweet that needs little sugar!

People bought certain cuts of meat from the butcher which were not rationed. They cooked meals with sheep's head, heart and brain, and pig's trotters.

SHEEP'S HEAD STEW

1 sheep's head, 1 sprig of mint, 2 carrots, 1 turnip, 1 onion,
1 teacup of pearl barley or rice, salt and pepper.

Wash a whole or half a head in strong salt water. Put into a saucepan with a sprig of mint, some carrots, a turnip, a diced onion and a teacup of pearl barley or rice. Cover with water, and add salt and pepper. Bring to the boil, remove all scum, turn down the gas and simmer gently for 3 to 4 hours. Remove the meat from the bones and return to the vegetable stock to reheat. Serve with onion sauce.

Posters encouraged people to eat more potatoes than bread, because people could grow their own potatoes.

DETECTIVE WORK

Hunt in junk shops and second-hand book shops, or at car-boot sales and antique fairs, for wartime recipe books. Then ask for help in cooking one of the recipes you find. You could try the recipe for Portman Pudding, which is written above.

DIGGING FOR VICTORY

To help with shortages, people were encouraged to grow their own vegetables. All areas of ground that could be made into vegetable plots, including school playing fields, lawns, flower gardens and tennis courts, were dug up and planted with crops. Even the moat at Hampton Court became a vegetable garden.

After August 1940, the government gave awards to people who grew crops in their garden all year round. Even the few centimetres of soil on the top of air-raid shelters in people's gardens were used, usually for growing marrows. Sometimes rhubarb and mushrooms were grown in tubs inside the shelter.

Again, the government published propaganda posters. People were told to 'Dig for Victory' and 'Make "Digging, Reaping, Saving" your gardening motto'.

Posters were used to show people when to plant certain crops. This one is for a vegetable garden in winter.

🐾 What sort of poster is this advertisement designed to look like?

Air-raid shelters were often covered in soil to give added protection. This woman, like many others, has planted vegetables on the top of her shelter.

These boys, from a school in Kent, are digging up potatoes to be used in the canteen.

DETECTIVE WORK

Look in second-hand bookshops for wartime gardening books, such as *The Weekend Gardener*, or magazines called *Garden Work* and *Gardeners' Chronicle*. You might also find wartime copies of the *Radio Times*, with listings for radio programmes such as *In Your Garden* and *The Kitchen Front*.

People were encouraged to cultivate allotments, as the newspaper notice below shows.

DEFENCE REGULATIONS 1939

WARTIME ALLOTMENTS

The Town Council desire to ascertain the number of people who would be prepared to cultivate allotments ... the rent charged will be as small as circumstances will permit. All those who are prepared to assist the national effort by cultivating an allotment are requested to send their names and addresses to the undersigned AT ONCE.

Percy Smallman, Town Clerk, Municipal Offices, Weymouth.
28th September, 1939

Allotments played an important part in keeping people fed, and anyone who damaged them was severely punished. During his research, Sherlock discovered that dog owners could be fined £5 if their animals strayed on to an allotment. Thieves were fined or sent to prison for stealing vegetables.

KEEPING ANIMALS

Before the Second World War it was common for people to keep a few chickens or rabbits in their backyards or gardens, to provide eggs and meat. When meat rationing began in March 1940, raising animals became an even more important way of providing extra food.

In 1945 it was estimated that 11.5 million chickens were being kept in gardens. People who had enough space sometimes kept goats for their milk and meat. In the countryside there were plenty of wild rabbits that could be trapped or shot, but rabbits were also bred in hutches to be eaten. All these animals could be fed on scraps, so they cost very little to keep.

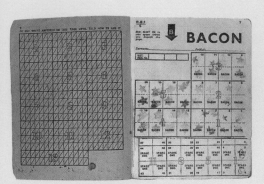

A ration book for bacon. Meat rationing increased the need for people to keep animals.

These ARP wardens are helping the National Food Scheme by keeping chickens at their ARP post in Hackney.

❖ What do you think the letters on the man's uniform and helmet might stand for?

These pigs were kept on Ilford Council's pig farm. They ate the scraps collected from canteens and restaurants.

This poster was used to ask people to save their kitchen waste, so that it could be fed to pigs.

Pigs were very popular, as they were cheap to keep and almost the whole animal could be eaten. People said that the only thing you could not use from a pig was its squeak.

Some people were able to keep pigs in their gardens, but other people joined a 'Pig Club'. They provided scraps to the farmer who fed the pig. In return, when the pig was killed they were given some of the meat. Councils also collected scraps from houses and passed them on to pig-keepers. In some areas this practice continued well into the 1950s.

DETECTIVE WORK

Interview any members of your family who lived through the war. Can they remember keeping animals for food during the war? You might be able to compare the different experiences of several relatives, especially if some lived in the country and others in towns.

CLOTHES RATIONING

Clothes rationing was introduced in June 1941. The scheme was kept secret up until the last minute, to prevent people rushing to the shops to buy clothes before rationing started. Everyone was given an allowance of 'coupons' or 'points', and each item of clothing was worth a certain number of coupons.

People could choose how to spend their points, depending on what new clothes they needed. Early in 1942, each person was given sixty coupons, which had to last for fifteen months.

This book of clothing coupons was issued to Annie Cann of Portsmouth.

CLOTHES RATIONS

60 coupons would mean a man could buy a total of the following.
1 pair of socks every 4 months.
1 pair of shoes every 8 months.
1 shirt every 20 months.
1 pair of trousers and 1 jacket every 2 years.
1 vest and 1 pair of pants every 2 years.
1 waistcoat every 5 years.
1 pullover every 5 years.
1 overcoat every 7 years.

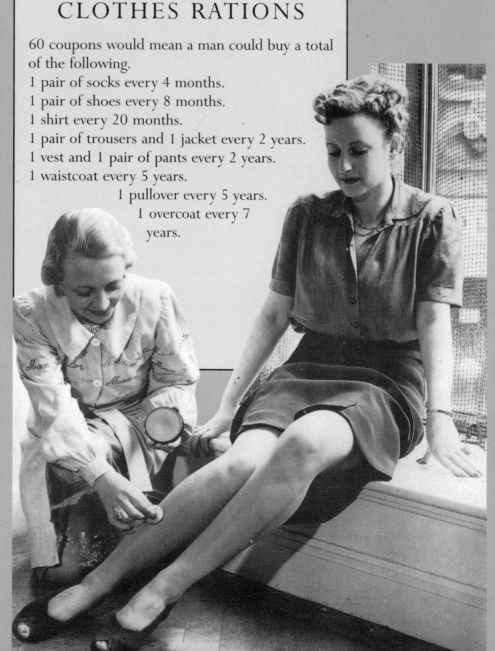

A woman at the beauty parlour.

❧ Why do you think this woman is having her legs painted?

This poster was used to persuade people to mend their clothes, rather than buying new ones.

These two evacuees, Isa Kelly and Betty Murphy, are seen wearing coats which were donated by Princess Elizabeth and Princess Margaret.

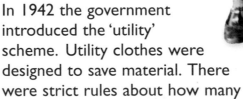

DETECTIVE WORK
Search through a second-hand book shop for books containing photographs of people in Britain during the war. Study them carefully, and see if you can spot the way people's clothes changed. You might be able to spot some home-made clothes or 'hand-me-downs'. Ask any relatives who lived through the war if they have a clothes ration book to add to your project.

In 1942 the government introduced the 'utility' scheme. Utility clothes were designed to save material. There were strict rules about how many buttonholes, pleats, seams and pockets these clothes could have, and how wide sleeves, hems and collars could be. Men's socks could not be more than 22 cm long. The price of utility clothes was controlled by the government. Utility coats for children cost 40 per cent less than normal coats.

❀ Why do you think utility clothes could not have many buttons, pleats and pockets?

The government used posters with slogans such as 'Make-do and mend' to persuade people to repair their clothes instead of throwing them away. It also offered advice on how children's clothes could be made from the material of adults' cast-offs and urged people to donate old clothes or 'hand-me-downs'.

SAVING FUEL

RATIONING OF PETROL

BOOKS OF COUPONS

SUPPLIES TO VARY WITH HORSE-POWER

As announced on Sunday night rationing of petrol will be introduced as from September 16. Until that date owners of motor-cars will be able to obtain supplies as at present except that petrol may be supplied by garages and service stations only into the tank of a vehicle. The Government expect cars to be used only for essential purposes.

❀ Read this article from 1939. Why do you think petrol was only supplied into the tank of a vehicle?

Because of petrol rationing, horses were once again used for basic transport needs. This picture shows a horse-drawn van in Regent Street, London.

The giant oil tankers that carried fuel across the Atlantic were an easy target for the German submarines. Britain desperately needed oil and other types of fuel for its ships, aircraft and factories. If these supplies had ever been completely cut off, Britain might have been forced out of the war.

Petrol rationing was introduced in September 1939. The monthly ration was so small that it could easily be used up in a day. Doctors, vets and other people who needed a car for their jobs were given extra rations. Other people, including some army regiments, travelled by bicycle or on horseback. After 1942, no petrol was allowed for private cars at all.

Despite petrol rationing, people could still buy new cars. In 1939, an Austin '10' could be yours for £175. Gas companies in London tried to introduce gas-propelled cars and there were various sites in London where these cars could be filled up with gas. But gas-powered cars never became very popular.

Britain had to ship in all of its oil, but it did have good supplies of coal. However, the government needed to save as much coal as possible for power stations, where it was used to produce electricity. The coal that people could use to heat their homes was rationed. From July 1941, each household was limited to one ton (1,016 kg) of coal each month.

People were asked to help the war effort by using less coal.

DETECTIVE WORK

Have a look through your telephone directory, or ask at the Tourist Information Centre, to try to find a local transport museum. Phone or visit the museum, and ask if they can help you find any information about unusual forms of transport used because of petrol rationing.

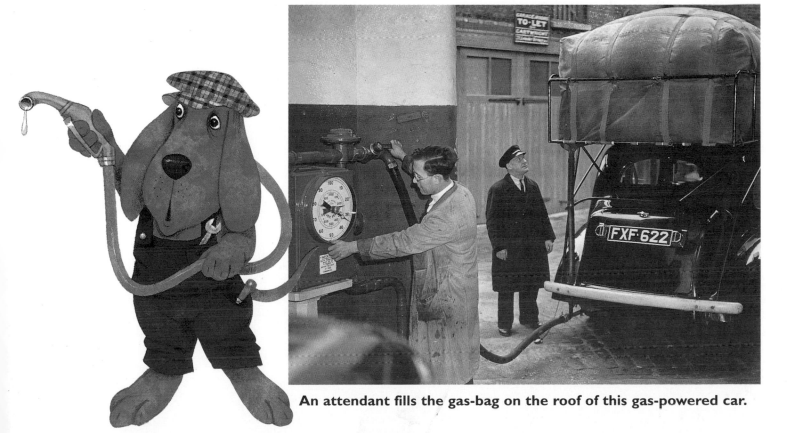

An attendant fills the gas-bag on the roof of this gas-powered car.

RECYCLING

Today, we are all encouraged to recycle as many products as possible. Recycling was important during the war, too, although it was not called by that name. On 11 July 1940, Lord Beaverbrook, the Minister of Aircraft Production, asked women to donate aluminium pots and pans so that they could be melted down and used for aircraft parts. Railings were also cut down and melted to provide a source of iron.

The Women's Voluntary Service (WVS) was put in charge of collecting pots and pans, and gathered 1,000 tonnes of them. However, only about 2 per cent of the donated pans were ever used. This became annoying later in the war, when it became very difficult to buy saucepans. The collection of metal items was in fact organized to make people feel they were helping the war effort. Most of the metal collected was unsuitable for recycling, and it had to be buried in large pits.

DORSET DAILY ECHO

15 July 1940

Excellent response to the recent appeal for aluminium ... Between 1,000 and 1,500 articles were received within two days of the appeal. Among the goods received are pots, pans, kettles, preserving pans, hot-water bottles, flasks, double boilers, saucepans, coffee pots, tea pots, boot trees, strainers and knitting needles.

Children help the war effort by recycling their old metal toys.

It was not only metal items that were recycled. The 'rag and bone man' travelled round the streets collecting rags, bones and paper. Paper was in very short supply, and envelopes had to be reused many times. Paperchases, like the one in the photograph below, were organized to collect scrap paper.

WELL, BOYS! IM FOR THE SHELL FACTORY!

AND IM FOR THE GLUE FACTORY!

AND ITS ME FOR MUNITIONS!

PAPER BONES RAGS

THE GREAT ROUND UP.
"WHEN WILL THESE THREE MEET AGAIN IN SHELLS, IN TANKS, OR IN PLANE?"

🐾 According to this poster, what were paper, bones and rags recycled for?

A paperchase in Croydon in 1941. Paper was thrown out of windows from shops and offices, and collected by the procession of volunteers.

DETECTIVE WORK

With a parent or teacher, look in your local area for evidence of where railings might have been removed for their metal. Old public buildings, churches and parks are good places to look. You can usually see part of the railing embedded in the brickwork or pavement. Take a camera with you to record your evidence.

YOUR PROJECT

If you have been following the Detective Work activities, you should now be able to track down enough clues to produce your own project about rationing. First you must decide on a topic to investigate. Choose one which you find interesting. You might find a topic by looking through this book's index. You could also use one of the following questions as a starting point.

These people are queuing to buy horse-meat, because other meat was rationed. Can you see the notice which says: 'Horse flesh passed for human consumption'? This meant it was safe to eat.

> ## Topic Questions
> - Where did people 'Dig for Victory' in your area? What did they grow?
> - How did people stay healthy on wartime rations?
> - What different products were rationed?
> - What kinds of clothes did people wear during the war?
> - How did people in your local area help with recycling?

You also need to think about how to present your project. Here are a few ideas.

Project Presentation

- Draw a map of your area, showing the land that was used for growing vegetables.
- Make a booklet of wartime recipes and tips for staying healthy.
- Make tapes of people talking about rationing and produce a radio programme.
- Produce a fashion magazine featuring wartime clothing and advertisements.
- Produce your own propaganda posters.

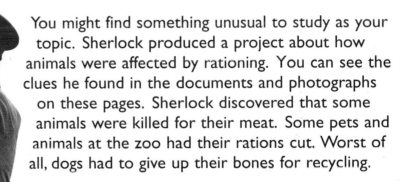

You might find something unusual to study as your topic. Sherlock produced a project about how animals were affected by rationing. You can see the clues he found in the documents and photographs on these pages. Sherlock discovered that some animals were killed for their meat. Some pets and animals at the zoo had their rations cut. Worst of all, dogs had to give up their bones for recycling.

This newspaper article (right) reveals that it was illegal to feed birds with food that was suitable for humans.

A keeper at London Zoo (left) feeds the pelicans. Even these big birds had their fish rations cut during the war.

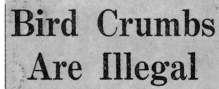

Bird Crumbs Are Illegal

CAGE PETS MUST BE CUT

By PERCY W. D. IZZARD

A MINISTRY OF FOOD official declared yesterday: "It is illegal to use bread, oatmeal, and other forms of human food for feeding cage birds and pigeons. It is also extremely unpatriotic."

He was referring to the recent decision to stop the importation of cage bird food, and consequent statements of bird fanciers that if they could not get bird seed they would use oatmeal and similar articles.

GLOSSARY

allotments Small pieces of land that people rent to grow crops on.

allowance The amount allowed to somebody.

armaments Military weapons and equipment.

convoys Groups of ships travelling together for safety.

coupons Small tickets that can be torn out of a ration book.

expectant mother A pregnant woman.

hand-me-downs Clothing passed from one person to another.

hoard Collect and store for future use.

imported Brought from other countries.

merchant ships Ships carrying goods.

microfilm Film on which documents can be stored in miniature.

ministry A government department.

munitions Weapons, ammunition and other military equipment.

oz Short for ounce, a measurement of weight equal to 28.34 grams.

propaganda Information used to make people think in a certain way.

quart A measurement of liquid equal to 1.136 litres.

rationing Allowing everyone a fixed amount of goods such as food, clothing and fuel.

recycling Converting waste into useful material.

squander Spend or use wastefully.

torpedoed Hit by a torpedo, a missile fired through the water.

utility Being useful, a useful thing.

BOOKS TO READ

Britain in World War II, Worksheets
by Martin Parsons (Wayland, 1998)
Sid's War by Jon Blake
(Franklin Watts, 1999)
War in the Countryside
by Sadie Ward (Cameron, 1988)
Wartime Cookbook by Anne and Brian Moses
(Wayland, 1995)

Wartime Country Kitchen and Garden
by Jennifer Davis (BBC Books, 1993)
Wartime Whiffs, Smelly Old History
by Mary Dobson (Oxford, 1999)
We'll Eat Again (a collection of recipes from the war years) by Marguerite Patten
(History in Evidence / Imperial War Museum, 1998)

Children can use this book to improve their literacy skills in the following ways:

✓ To identify the purpose of recipes, and to write recipes as instructional text using organizational devices (Year 3, Term 2, non-fiction reading comprehension and writing composition).

✓ To identify newspaper features, predict newspaper stories from headlines, and to write newspaper-style reports (Year 4, Term 1, non-fiction reading comprehension and writing composition).

✓ To evaluate government advertisements for their impact, appeal and honesty (Year 4, Term 3, non-fiction reading comprehension).

✓ To design an advertisement, such as a rationing poster (Year 4, Term 3, writing composition).

Page 5:
❀ Bacon, butter and ham were rationed at the start of the war.
❀ There were three types of ration book: a general book (for men, women and children over six years old), a child's book (for children under six) and a traveller's book (for those who did not live at home permanently).
❀ 'Dig for Victory' means to grow more food to help the war effort. The 'Dig for Victory' campaign was introduced in 1939 as the 'Grow More Food Campaign'. It was designed to get people to grow food in gardens and allotments. 'Dig for Victory' was used as a more catchy slogan.

Page 6:
❀ This ration book was issued in Wandsworth on 23 October 1939.

Page 7:
❀ There was a paper shortage, and it saved paper to use a smaller coupon. It was also quicker to simply draw a line through it, rather than cut it out.

Page 8:
❀ Although fish was not rationed, the shop only had a limited amount. The shopkeeper did not want people from outside the area buying all the fish, leaving none for the local customers. He could prevent this by checking identity cards, because they had people's addresses on them.

Page 9:
❀ People could get an extra sugar allowance if they made marmalade, manufactured sweets, chocolates or cakes, or kept bees!

Page 12:
❀ The symbol is a swastika, which was a symbol of the Nazis. It was used to show that squandering anything was helping Germany.

Page 14:
❀ It was important to be able to see in the dark because of the 'blackout', when lights were switched off at night to make it difficult for enemy bombers to see their targets.
❀ If children can buy oranges today and tomorrow, but adults have to wait until Wednesday, it must be two days before Wednesday – so it is Monday.

Page 14 (continued):
❀ Children under six were allowed to buy oranges. This was because they were thought to need vitamin C more than older people.
❀ If children bought all the oranges before Wednesday, then adults would have to do without.

Page 15:
❀ A doctor, certified midwife or health visitor could sign the application form of an expectant mother.

Page 16:
❀ The posters on the wall include (far left) the Dig for Victory poster from page 5 of this book; an advertisement for milk in the centre; and two Potato Pete advertisements on the bottom-right, encouraging people to eat potatoes. Above Potato Pete there are advertisements for markets and bread, and a warning against waste.

Page 18:
❀ It is designed to look like a theatre poster, advertising its stars.

Page 20:
❀ The 'W' on his helmet stands for Warden. The ARP on his uniform badge stands for Air Raid Precautions, the organization which planned defence against air raids.

Page 22:
❀ Stockings were difficult to obtain, so the woman is having her legs covered in a special make-up, the same colour as stockings. Some women used an eyebrow pencil to draw a line up the back of their legs, to look like the seam of a stocking.

Page 23:
❀ Pockets and pleats used a lot of material, so utility clothes were made with fewer pockets and no pleats. Buttons were also in short supply, so fewer were used.

Page 24:
❀ Petrol was supplied only into the tanks of vehicles to stop people collecting extra supplies in containers.

Page 27:
❀ According to the poster, paper was used in shell factories, bones were made into glue, and rags were used in munitions factories.

INDEX

Numbers in bold refer to pictures and captions.